D1564310

THE IRISH FOR NO

CIARÁN CARSON

THE IRISH
FOR NO.

WAKE FOREST UNIVERSITY PRESS

THE GALLERY PRESS

Published in North America by Wake Forest University Press in November,
1987. Text designed by Peter Fallon and published in Ireland by Gallery
Press (19 Oakdown Road, Dublin 14) in July, 1987.

ISBN-0-916390-29-2

LC Card Number 87-050730

Acknowledgements

The author is grateful to John Campbell of Mullaghbawn whose
storytelling suggested some of the narrative procedures of some of these
poems; and to Michael Foley for reminding him of what Frank Ifield
really sang.

Contents

Turn Again

There is a map of the city which shows the bridge that was
   never built.
A map which shows the bridge that collapsed; the streets that
   never existed.
Ireland's Entry, Elbow Lane, Weigh-house Lane, Back Lane,
   Stone-Cutter's Entry –
Today's plan is already yesterday's – the streets that were there
   are gone.
And the shape of the jails cannot be shown for security reasons.

The linen backing is falling apart – the Falls Road hangs by a
   thread.
When someone asks me where I live, I remember where I
   used to live.
Someone asks me for directions, and I think again. I turn into
A side-street to try to throw off my shadow, and history is
   changed.

PART ONE

Dresden

Horse Boyle was called Horse Boyle because of his brother
Mule;
Though why Mule was called Mule is anybody's guess. I
stayed there once,
Or rather, I nearly stayed there once. But that's another story.
At any rate they lived in this decrepit caravan, not two miles
out of Carrick,
Encroached upon by baroque pyramids of empty baked bean
tins, rusts
And ochres, hints of autumn merging into twilight. Horse
believed
They were as good as a watchdog, and to tell you the truth
You couldn't go near the place without something falling over:
A minor avalanche would ensue – more like a shop bell, really,

The old-fashioned ones on string, connected to the latch,
I think,
And as you entered in, the bell would tinkle in the empty shop,
a musk
Of soap and turf and sweets would hit you from the gloom.
Tobacco.
Baling wire. Twine. And, of course, shelves and pyramids of
tins.
An old woman would appear from the back – there was a
sizzling pan in there,
Somewhere, a whiff of eggs and bacon – and ask you what you
wanted;
Or rather, she wouldn't ask; she would talk about the weather.
It had rained
That day, but it was looking better. They had just put in the
spuds.
I had only come to pass the time of day, so I bought a token
packet of Gold Leaf.

All this time the fry was frying away. Maybe she'd a daughter in there
Somewhere, though I hadn't heard the neighbours talk of it; if anybody knew,
It would be Horse. Horse kept his ears to the ground.
And he was a great man for current affairs; he owned the only TV in the place.
Come dusk he'd set off on his rounds, to tell the whole townland the latest
Situation in the Middle East, a mortar bomb attack in Mullaghbawn –
The damn things never worked, of course – and so he'd tell the story
How in his young day it was very different. Take young Flynn, for instance,
Who was ordered to take this bus and smuggle some sticks of gelignite

Across the border, into Derry, when the RUC – or was it the RIC? –
Got wind of it. The bus was stopped, the peeler stepped on. Young Flynn
Took it like a man, of course: he owned up right away. He opened the bag
And produced the bomb, his rank and serial number. For all the world
Like a pound of sausages. Of course, the thing was, the peeler's bike
Had got a puncture, and he didn't know young Flynn from Adam. All he wanted
Was to get home for his tea. Flynn was in for seven years and learned to speak
The best of Irish. He had thirteen words for a cow in heat;

A word for the third thwart in a boat, the wake of a boat on the
    ebb tide.

He knew the extinct names of insects, flowers, why this place
    was called
Whatever: *Carrick*, for example, was *a rock*. He was damn right
    there –
As the man said, *When you buy meat you buy bones, when you buy
    land you buy stones.*
You'd be hard put to find a square foot in the whole bloody
    parish
That wasn't thick with flints and pebbles. To this day he could
    hear the grate
And scrape as the spade struck home, for it reminded him of
    ⸴broken bones:
Digging a graveyard, maybe – or better still, trying to dig a
    reclaimed tip
Of broken delph and crockery ware – you know that sound that
    sets your teeth on edge
When the chalk squeaks on the blackboard, or you shovel ashes
    from the stove?

Master McGinty – he'd be on about McGinty then, and
    discipline, the capitals
Of South America, Moore's *Melodies*, the Battle of Clontarf,
    and
*Tell me this, an educated man like you: What goes on four legs when it's
    young,*
Two legs when it's grown up, and three legs when it's old? I'd pretend
I didn't know. McGinty's leather strap would come up then,
    stuffed
With threepenny bits to give it weight and sting. Of course, it
    never did him

Any harm: *You could take a horse to water but you couldn't make him drink.*
He himself was nearly going on to be a priest.
And many's the young cub left the school, as wise as when he came.

Carrowkeel was where McGinty came from – *Narrow Quarter,*
   Flynn explained –
Back before the Troubles, a place that was so mean and
   crabbed,
Horse would have it, men were known to eat their dinner from a
   drawer.
Which they'd slide shut the minute you'd walk in.
He'd demonstrate this at the kitchen table, hunched and
   furtive, squinting
Out the window – past the teetering minarets of rust, down the
   hedge-dark aisle –
To where a stranger might appear, a passer-by, or what was
   maybe worse,
Someone he knew. Someone who wanted something. Someone
   who was hungry.
Of course who should come tottering up the lane that instant
   but his brother

Mule. I forgot to mention they were twins. They were as like
   two –
No, not peas in a pod, for this is not the time nor the place to
   go into
Comparisons, and this is really Horse's story, Horse who – now
   I'm getting
Round to it – flew over Dresden in the war. He'd emigrated
   first, to
Manchester. Something to do with scrap – redundant mill
   machinery,

Giant flywheels, broken looms that would, eventually, be ships,
   or aeroplanes.
He said he wore his fingers to the bone.
And so, on impulse, he had joined the RAF. He became a rear
   gunner.
Of all the missions, Dresden broke his heart. It reminded him
   of china.

As he remembered it, long afterwards, he could hear, or almost
   hear
Between the rapid desultory thunderclaps, a thousand tinkling
   echoes –
All across the map of Dresden, store-rooms full of china
   shivered, teetered
And collapsed, an avalanche of porcelain, slushing and
   cascading: cherubs,
Shepherdesses, figurines of Hope and Peace and Victory,
   delicate bone fragments.
He recalled in particular a figure from his childhood, a
   milkmaid
Standing on the mantelpiece. Each night as they knelt down
   for the rosary,
His eyes would wander up to where she seemed to beckon to
   him, smiling,
Offering him, eternally, her pitcher of milk, her mouth of rose
   and cream.

One day, reaching up to hold her yet again, his fingers
   stumbled, and she fell.
He lifted down a biscuit tin, and opened it.
It breathed an antique incense: things like pencils, snuff,
   tobacco.
His war medals. A broken rosary. And there, the milkmaid's

creamy hand, the outstretched
Pitcher of milk, all that survived. Outside, there was a scraping
And a tittering; I knew Mule's step by now, his careful drunken
   weaving
Through the tin-stacks. I might have stayed the night, but
   there's no time
To go back to that now; I could hardly, at any rate, pick up
   the thread.
I wandered out through the steeples of rust, the gate that was
   a broken bed.

Judgement

The tarred road simmered in a blue haze. The reservoir was dry.
The railway sleepers oozed with creosote. Not a cloud to be seen in the
  sky

We were sitting at the Camlough halt – Johnny Mickey and
  myself – waiting
For a train that never seemed to come. He was telling me this
  story
Of a Father Clarke, who wanted to do in his dog. A black and
  white terrier.
He says to the servant boy, *Take out that old bitch*, he says, *and
  drown her.*
Johnny Mickey said the servant boy was Quigley, and now
  that he remembered it,
He'd been arrested by a Sergeant Flynn, for having no bell on
  his bike.
Hardly a hanging crime, you might say. But he was fined
  fifteen shillings.

The prisoner left the court-room and his step was long and slow
By day and night he did contrive to fill this sergeant's heart with woe

So there was this auction one day, and Quigley sneaks in the
  back.
A lot of crockery ware came up. Delph bowls. Willow-pattern.
  Chamberpots.
The bidding started at a shilling. Quigley lifts his finger. One-
  and-six.
Everyone pretending not to look at one another. Or to know
  each other.
Nods and winks. A folded *Dundalk Democrat*. Spectacles put on
  and off.
And so on, till he won the bid at fifteen shillings. *Name, please,*

Says the auctioneer. *Sergeant Flynn,* says Quigley, *Forkhill Barracks.*

For to uphold the letter of the law this sergeant was too willing
I took the law upon myself and fined him back his fifteen shillings

He rambled on a bit – how this Flynn's people on his mother's side
Were McErleans from County Derry, how you could never trust
A McErlean. When they hanged young McCorley on the bridge of Toome
It was a McErlean who set the whole thing up. That was in '98,
But some things never changed. You could trust a dog but not a cat.
It was something in their nature, and nature, as they say, will out.
The pot would always call the kettle black. He hummed a few lines.

Come tender-hearted Christians all attention pay to me
Till I relate and communicate these verses two or three
Concerning of a gallant youth was cut off in his bloom
And died upon the gallows tree near to the town of Toome

Which brought Johnny Mickey back to the priest and the terrier bitch.
Quigley, it transpired, had walked the country – Ballinliss and Aughaduff,
Slievenacapall, Carnavaddy – looking for a place to drown her.
It was the hottest summer in living memory. Not a cloud to be seen in the sky.
The Cully Water was a trickle. The Tullyallen and the Ummeracam were dry.

Not a breath of wind. Not so much water as would drown a rat.
　After three days
Quigley and the bitch came back. They were both half-dead
　with thirst.

He looked her up he looked her down in his heart was ne'er a pang
I'll tell you what says Father Clarke if she won't be drowned she'll hang

Johnny Mickey said that priests had a great way with ropes and
　knots.
It was one of the tricks that they learned in the seminary.
　Something to do
With chasubles and albs. In less time than it takes to tell,
　Father Flynn
Had rigged up a noose. They brought the bitch out to the
　orchard
And strung her up from the crook of an apple tree. And who
　was passing by
But the poet McCooey. He peeped through a hole in the hedge.
He spotted the two boys at their trade, and this is what he
　said:

A man with no bell on his bike a man with a single bed
It's hardly any wonder that you'd go off your head
Poor old bitch poor old friend you died without a bark
Sentenced by Johnny Quigley and hung by Father Clarke

Of course, said Johnny Mickey, your man McCooey's long
　since dead.
A white plume of steam appeared around the bend. A long
　lonesome blast.
The tracks began to shimmer and to hum. Our train was
　coming in
And not a minute late. It shivered to a halt. We both got on.

We would pass the crazy map of a dried-up reservoir. A water-
    tower.
We would watch the telegraph lines float up and down, till we
    arrived
At the other end; I would hand Mickey Quigley over to the
    two attendants.

Farewell unto you sweet Drumaul if in you I had stayed
Among the Presbyterians I ne'er would have been betrayed
The gallows tree I ne'er would have seen had I remained there
For Dufferin you betrayed me McErlean you set the snare

Calvin Klein's Obsession

I raised my glass, and – solid, pungent, like the soot-encrusted
    brickwork
Of the Ulster Brewery – a smell of yeast and hops and malt
    swam up:
I sniff and sniff again, and try to think of what it is I am remembering:
I think that's how it goes, like Andy Warhol's calendar of
    perfumes,
Dribs and drabs left over to remind him of that season's smell.
Very personal, of course, as *Blue Grass* is for me the texture of a
    fur
Worn by this certain girl I haven't seen in years. Every time
    that *Blue Grass*
Hits me, it is 1968. I'm walking with her through the smoggy
    early dusk
Of West Belfast: coal-smoke, hops, fur, the smell of stout and
    whiskey
Breathing out from somewhere. So it all comes back, or nearly
    all,
A long-forgotten kiss.

Never quite. Horses' dung is smoking on the cobbles.
    Cobblestones?
I must have gone back further than I thought, to brewers'
    drays and milk-carts,
Brylcreem, *Phoenix* beer. Or candy apples – rich hard dark-
    brown glaze
Impossible to bite at first, until you licked and licked and
    sucked a way
Into the soft core. A dark interior, where I'd also buy a twist of
    snuff
For my grandma. She'd put two pinches on a freckled fist, and
    sniff.
Then a sip of whiskey, and, as always, *I'm not long for this world.*
My father would make a face: *a whingeing gate*, he'd say, *hangs*

longest –
Hoping it was true, perhaps – a phrase he'd said so often, he'd
    forgotten
When he said it last. That *Gold Label* whiskey – nearly like a
    perfume:
I go crazy because I want to smell them all so much,

Warhol's high-pitched New York whine comes on again, with
All those exhalations of the 'thirties and the 'forties: Guerlain's
Sous le Vent, Saravel's *White Christmas,* Corday's *Voyage à Paris,*
    or
Kathleen Mary Quinlan's *Rhythm*: bottles of bottle-green,
    bruise-blues
Darker than the pansies at the cemetery gate-lodge, bottles of
    frosted glass
And palest lilac – *l'odeur de ton sein chaleureux* – a rush of musk
And incense, camphor, beckons from the back of the wardrobe;
    I'd slipped
Through the mirror in a dream. *Opium* by Yves St Laurent?
    More than likely,
What my mother used to call a guilty conscience, or something
    that I ate:
Cheese and chopped dill pickle on wheaten farls, looking, if I
    thought of it,
Like Boots' *Buttermilk and Clover* soap –

Slipping and slipping from my grasp, clunking softly
    downwards through
The greying water; I have drowsed off into something else.
    The ornate fish
And frog and water-lily motif on the bathroom wallpaper
    reminds me
How in fact I'd stripped it off some months ago. It was April,
    a time

Of fits and starts; fresh leaves blustered at the window, strips
and fronds
Of fish and water-lilies sloughed off round my feet. A Frank
Ifield song
From 1963, I think, kept coming back to me: *I remember you –
you're the one
Who made my dreams come true – just a few – kisses ago.* I'm taking
One step forward, two steps back, trying to establish what it
was about her
That made me fall in love with her, if that's what it was; *infatuation*
Was a vogue word then –

It meant it wasn't all quite real. Like looking at my derelict
back garden,
Its scraggy ranks of docks and nettles, thistles, but thinking
There was something else, flicking idly through the pages of a
catalogue:
Flowered violets and whites, or grey and silver foliage,
suggesting
Thunderclouds and snowstorms, rivers, fountains; artemesias
and lilies,
Phlox, gentians, scillas, snowdrops, crocuses; and thymes and
camomiles
Erupted from the paving-cracks, billowing from half-forgotten
corners;
An avalanche of jasmine and wisteria broke through. Or, the
perfume
Of *Blue Grass*, bittersweet, which is, just at this moment, just
a memory.
How often did she wear it, anyway? I must look her up again
some day.
And can it still be bought?

For there are memories that have no name; you don't know
  what to ask for.
The merest touch of sunshine, a sudden breeze, might summon
  up
A corner of your life you'd thought, till then, you'd never
  occupied.
Her mother, for example, owned this second-hand shop, which
  is where
The fur coat came from, anonymous with shades of someone
  else. Rummaging
Through piles of coats and dresses, I'd come across a thing
  that until then
I'd never wanted: a white linen 'fifties jacket with no back vent,
Just that bit out of fashion, it was fashionable, or maybe, as
  they say,
It was just the thing I had been looking for. So, a box of worn
  shoes
Might bring me back to 1952, teetering across the kitchen
  floor
In my mother's high heels –

Not that I wanted to be her; easing off the lid of her powder
  compact,
Breathing in the flesh-coloured dust, was just a way of feeling
  her presence.
And so I have this image of an assignation, where it all comes
  back,
Or nearly all, a long-forgotten kiss: subdued lighting, musak –
  no, a live
Piano – tinkling in its endless loop; there is candlelight and
  Cointreau,
Whispered nothings, as Kathleen Mary Quinlan's *Rhythm*
  meets, across

A discreet table, Calvin Klein's *Obsession.* He has prospered
    since
He saw her last. There is talk of all the years that separated
    them, whatever
Separated them at first. There is talk of money, phrased as
    talk of
Something else, of how there are some things that can't be
    bought.
Or maybe it's the name you buy, and not the thing itself.

Whatever Sleep It Is

The leg was giving me a problem, interfering, somehow, with
    the total
Composition – I didn't know, at this stage, if he'd be a walker
    or a skier.
Certainly, a far-away look in his eyes suggested mountain
    scenery, the light
Falling gradually, then pouring as an avalanche across a great
    divide:
Cuckoo-clocks and cow-bells, everything as full of holes as a
    Swiss cheese.
And I wanted to give him a leather jacket – leather is
    'interesting' though
Sometimes it's easy and sometimes not, depending on the time
    of day, the light,
The consistency of this particular tube of burnt sienna. So if it
    doesn't work
It might be tweed. But then the air of mystery might vanish,
    this spy
Or pilot whose whereabouts have yet to be established –

At any rate, I painted out the leg, and put in this flight of stairs
    instead.
It seemed to me it should lead to a skylight, so dusty as to be
    opaque,
Cobwebbed, opening with a slow reluctant creak – the see-saw
    of a donkey –
On to clouds and bits of sky. A gusty March day, maybe, with
    a touch of rain
Ticking on the glass. Someone keeps asking me why I hold my
    hand like that,
But it's not to keep off the light – it's more to do with how you
    often
Don't remember what a hand looks like. So you paint your own,
    and give it

To this character who might, indeed, be you, but with a life
   you haven't
Worked out yet. The sleeve of your jacket ticked with sky-blue,
   Chinese white.
I think the story is starting to take shape:

It usually takes three days, four days, and you can reckon on
   a week
Before it's finished. On the seventh day I'd go out on the town
   and celebrate,
And then come back and look at it again: sometimes I'd say
   yes, sometimes no.
On day five, for instance, the skylight acquired a broken
   pane, and someone
Had to be responsible: I thought of a message wrapped around
   a stone.
What was being said, and why? Could it be that the character
   I'd painted out
By now was lurking out there? Perhaps he is in love with this
   girl
Hunched in the attic, where the light-source now becomes a
   candle
Stuck in a Chianti bottle, a love that tells itself by paper,
   stone, scissors.
And the donkey keeps coming back,

Its too-big head lolling over a five-barred gate that opens out
   on to
An orchard: there is, in fact, a bowl of apples at her elbow that
   she seems
To be ignoring. It is there to concentrate the light, I think –
   flecks
And smuts of amber, yellow, russet, green, each fruit swirled
   into a fist,

The navel clenched between the finger and the thumb.
Meanwhile Mr Natural,
As we'll call him, has climbed on to the roof, and, with his feet
    lodged
In the guttering, is staring through the hole at her. *The pane of
    glass*
I skimmed this morning from the drinking-trough, he whispers to
    himself,
Melted, and I let it fall and break. Early frost: the stars are blazing
Now like snowflakes – stem end and blossom end

Swelling and dimming over the black Alp of the roof. It is an
    October
Sort of March, the apples ripened out of season; and now that
    the ink-dark sky
Lightens into sapphire, I see it is an angel, not a man, who has
Descended, looking faintly puzzled at the poor response of the
    girl
To whatever important announcement he has just made. She
    is, in fact, asleep,
Oblivious also to the clink and hum of the electric milk float
Which has just pulled up outside. And the milkman looks up,
    momentarily
Amazed at curtains, wings, gusting from the attic window. He
    rubs his eyes;
He is still drowsy with these six days out of seven. Tomorrow
    yawns ahead
With routine promises; tomorrow, after all, he will be free.

PART TWO

Belfast Confetti

Suddenly as the riot squad moved in, it was raining
  exclamation marks,
Nuts, bolts, nails, car-keys. A fount of broken type. And the
  explosion
Itself – an asterisk on the map. This hyphenated line, a burst of
  rapid fire . . .
I was trying to complete a sentence in my head, but it kept
  stuttering,
All the alleyways and side-streets blocked with stops and
  colons.

I know this labyrinth so well – Balaclava, Raglan, Inkerman,
  Odessa Street –
Why can't I escape? Every move is punctuated. Crimea Street.
  Dead end again.
A Saracen, Kremlin-2 mesh. Makrolon face-shields. Walkie-
  talkies. What is
My name? Where am I coming from? Where am I going? A
  fusillade of question-marks.

Clearance

The Royal Avenue Hotel collapses under the breaker's
    pendulum:
Zig-zag stairwells, chimney-flues, and a 'thirties mural
Of an elegantly-dressed couple doing what seems to be the
    Tango, in Wedgewood
Blue and white – happy days! Suddenly more sky
Than there used to be. A breeze springs up from nowhere –

There, through a gap in the rubble, a greengrocer's shop
I'd never noticed until now. Or had I passed it yesterday?
    Everything –
Yellow, green and purple – is fresh as paint. Rain glistens on the
    aubergines
And peppers; even from this distance, the potatoes smell of
    earth.

Linear B

Threading rapidly between crowds on Royal Avenue, reading
Simultaneously, and writing in this black notebook, peering
  through
A cracked lens fixed with Sellotape, his *rendez-vous* is not quite
  vous.
But from years of watching, I know the zig-zags circle:
He has been the same place many times, never standing still.

One day I clicked with his staccato walk, and glimpsed the
  open notebook:
Squiggles, dashes, question-marks, dense as the Rosetta stone.
His good eye glittered at me: it was either nonsense, or a
  formula – for
Perpetual motion, the scaffolding of shopping lists, or the
  collapsing city.

Night Patrol

Jerking his head spasmodically as he is penetrated by invisible
  gunfire,
The private wakes to a frieze of pull-outs from *Contact* and
  Men Only.
Sellotape and Blu-Tack. The antiquated plumbing is stuttering
  that he
Is not in Balkan Street or Hooker Street, but in a bunk bed
In the Grand Central Hotel: a room that is a room knocked into
  other rooms.

But the whole Victorian creamy façade has been tossed off
To show the inner-city tubing: cables, sewers, a snarl of
  Portakabins,
Soft-porn shops and carry-outs. A Telstar Taxis depot that is a
  hole
In a breeze-block wall, a wire grille and a voice-box uttering
  gobbledygook.

August 1969

As the huge façade of Greeves's Mill is washed in a Niagara of
  flame
The riot fizzles out. Still smouldering as the troops march in,
  this welcome,
Singing, dancing on the streets. Confetti drifts across the city:
Charred receipts and bills-of-lading, contracts, dockets, pay-
  slips.
The weave is set: a melt of bobbins, spindles, shuttles.

Happy days, my mother claims, the mill-girls chattering,
  linking arms.
But then, it all changed when I met your father. The flicker of a
  smile.
It lights again on this creased photograph, a weekend
  honeymoon.
She is crossing the Liffey, the indelible ink of *Dublin
  September 1944.*

Campaign

They had questioned him for hours. Who exactly was he?
  And when
He told them, they questioned him again. When they accepted
  who he was, as
Someone not involved, they pulled out his fingernails. Then
They took him to a waste-ground somewhere near the
  Horseshoe Bend, and told him
What he was. They shot him nine times.

A dark umbilicus of smoke was rising from a heap of burning
  tyres.
The bad smell he smelt was the smell of himself. Broken glass
  and knotted Durex.
The knuckles of a face in a nylon stocking. I used to see him in
  the Gladstone Bar,
Drawing pints for strangers, his almost-perfect fingers flecked
  with scum.

Smithfield Market

Sidelong to the arcade, the glassed-in April cloud – fleeting,
    pewter-edged –
Gets lost in shadowed aisles and inlets, branching into
    passages, into cul-de-sacs,
Stalls, compartments, alcoves. Everything unstitched,
    unravelled – mouldy fabric,
Rusted heaps of nuts and bolts, electrical spare parts: the
    ammunition dump
In miniature. Maggots seethe between the ribs and
    corrugations.

Since everything went up in smoke, no entrances, no exits.
But as the charred beams hissed and flickered, I glimpsed a
    map of Belfast
In the ruins: obliterated streets, the faint impression of a key.
Something many-toothed, elaborate, stirred briefly in the
    labyrinth.

Army

The duck patrol is waddling down the odd-numbers side of
   Raglan Street,
The bass-ackwards private at the rear trying not to think of a
   third eye
Being drilled in the back of his head. Fifty-five. They stop.
   The head
Peers round, then leaps the gap of Balaclava Street. He waves
   the body over
One by one. Forty-nine. Cape Street. A gable wall. Garnet
   Street. A gable wall.

Frere Street. Forty-seven. Forty-five-and-a-half. Milan Street.
   A grocer's shop.
They stop. They check their guns. Thirteen. Milton Street. An
   iron lamp-post.
Number one. Ormond Street. *Two ducks in front of a duck and
   two ducks*
Behind a duck, how many ducks? Five? *No. Three.* This is not the end.

33333

I was trying to explain to the invisible man behind the wire-
grilled
One-way mirror and squawk-box exactly where it was I
wanted to go, except
I didn't know myself – a number in the Holy Land, Damascus
Street or Cairo?
At any rate in about x amount of minutes, where x is a small
number,
I found myself in the synthetic leopard-skin bucket-seat of a
Ford Zephyr

Gunning through a mesh of ramps, diversions, one-way
systems. We shoot out
Under the glare of the sodium lights along the blank brick wall
of the Gasworks
And I start to ease back: I know this place like the back of my
hand, except
My hand is cut off at the wrist. We stop at an open door I
never knew existed.

Two Winos

Most days you will find this pair reclining on the waste ground
Between Electric Street and Hemp Street, sharing a bottle of
  Drawbridge
British Wine. They stare at isolated clouds, or puffs of steam
  which leak out
From the broken pipes and vents at the back of the Franklin
  Laundry . . .
They converse in snarls and giggles, and they understand each
  other perfectly.

Just now they have entered the giggling phase, though what
  there is
To laugh at, who knows. Unless it was this momentary ray of
  sunlight
That glanced across their patch of crushed coke, broken glass
  and cinders;
And the bottle which had seemed half-empty until then is now
  half-full.

Cocktails

Bombing at about ninety miles an hour with the exhaust
  skittering
The skid-marked pitted tarmac of Kennedy Way, they hit the
  ramp and sailed
Clean over the red-and-white guillotine of the check-point
  and landed
On the M1 flyover, then disappeared before the Brits knew
  what hit them. So
The story went: we were in the Whip and Saddle bar of the
  Europa.

There was talk of someone who was shot nine times and lived,
  and someone else
Had the inside info. on the Romper Room. We were trying to
  remember the facts
Behind the Black & Decker case, when someone ordered
  another drink and we entered
The realm of Jabberwocks and Angels' Wings, Widows'
  Kisses, Corpse Revivers.

Travellers

On the waste ground that was Market Street and Verner
   Street, wandering trouserless
Through his personal map – junked refrigerators, cars and
   cookers, anchored
Caravans – the small boy trips over an extended tow-bar, picks
   himself up, giggles
And pisses on a smouldering mound of *Pampers*. *Sic transit
   gloria mundi* –
This is the exact site, now that I recall it, of Murdock's stables,
   past tense.

Murdock himself moved out to the *Flying Horse* estate some
   years ago. He wanted
To end his days among friends; there were Murdocks in the
   local graveyard.
The long umbilicus of dung between his back yard and
   Downpatrick faded. Belfast
Tore itself apart and patched things up again. Like this. Like
   his extended family.

Box

I can't sleep as long as I see this man with a cardboard box
   perched
On his head – no hands, his body bent into the *S* or *Z* of a
   snake-charmer's
Rope. HP Sauce, Heinz Baked Beans or Crosse & Blackwell's
   Cock-a-Leekie?
Hen-stepping out of a pea-soup fog, he makes a shift for
   Cornmarket
And pops up again in Smithfield: has he discarded this box
   for another?

In all these years, don't ask me what was in there: that would
   take
A bird's-eye view. But I get a whiff of homelessness, a scaldy
   fallen
From a nest into another nest, a cross between a toothbrush
   and a razor.
Open-mouthed, almost sleeping now. A smell of meths and
   cardboard.

Snowball

All the signs: beehive hair-do, white handbag, white stilettos,
    split skirt.
An Audi Quattro sidles up in first gear past the loading-bay of
    Tomb Street
GPO – a litter of white plastic cord, a broken whiskey bottle –
Then revs away towards the Albert Clock. The heels click off –
    another
Blind date? Like a fish-net stocking, everything is full of
    holes . . .

Arse-about-face, night-shift and the Christmas rush, perfume
    oozing from
Crushed packets – *Blue Grass*, *Obsession* – and once, in a
    forgotten pigeon-hole,
I woke up to this card stamped 9 August 1910: *Meet me usual
    place & time*
Tomorrow – What I have to tell you might not wait – Yours – Forever – B.

The Exiles' Club

Every Thursday in the upstairs lounge of the Wollongong Bar,
    they make
Themselves at home with Red Heart Stout, Park Drive
    cigarettes and Dunville's whiskey,
A slightly-mouldy batch of soda farls. Eventually, they get
    down to business.
After years they have reconstructed the whole of the Falls Road,
    and now
Are working on the back streets: Lemon, Peel and Omar,
    Balaclava, Alma.

They just about keep up with the news of bombings and
    demolition, and are
Struggling with the finer details: the names and dates carved
    out
On the back bench of the Leavers' Class in Slate Street School;
    the Nemo Café menu;
The effects of the 1941 Blitz, the entire contents of Paddy
    Lavery's pawnshop.

Slate Street School

Back again. Day one. Fingers blue with cold. I joined the
  lengthening queue.
Roll-call. Then inside: chalk-dust and iced milk, the smell of
  watered ink.
Roods, perches, acres, ounces, pounds, tons weighed
  imponderably in the darkening
Air. We had chanted the twelve-times table for the twelfth or
  thirteenth time
When it began to snow. Chalky numerals shimmered down; we
  crowded to the window –

*These are the countless souls of purgatory, whose numbers constantly
  diminish*
*And increase; each flake as it brushes to the ground is yet another soul
  released.*
And I am the avenging Archangel, stooping over mills and
  factories and barracks.
I will bury the dark city of Belfast forever under snow: inches,
  feet, yards, chains, miles.

PART THREE

The Irish for No

Was it a vision, or a waking dream? I heard her voice before I saw
What looked like the balcony scene in *Romeo and Juliet*, except
    Romeo
Seemed to have shinned up a pipe and was inside arguing with
    her. The casements
Were wide open and I could see some Japanese-style wall-
    hangings, the dangling
Quotation marks of a yin-yang mobile. *It's got nothing,* she was
    snarling, *nothing*
To do with politics, and, before the bamboo curtain came down,
That goes for you too!

It was time to turn into the dog's-leg short-cut from Chlorine
    Gardens
Into Cloreen Park, where you might see an *Ulster Says No*
    scrawled on the side
Of the power-block – which immediately reminds me of the
    Eglantine Inn
Just on the corner: on the missing *h* of Cloreen, you might say.
    We were debating,
Bacchus and the pards and me, how to render *The Ulster Bank –
    the Bank*
That Likes to Say Yes into Irish, and whether eglantine was alien
    to Ireland.
I cannot see what flowers are at my feet, when *yes* is the verb repeated,
Not exactly yes, but phatic nods and whispers. *The Bank That
    Answers All*
Your Questions, maybe? That Greek portico of Mourne granite,
    dazzling
With promises and feldspar, mirrors you in the Delphic black
    of its windows.

And the bruised pansies of the funeral parlour are dying in
    reversed gold letters,

The long sigh of the afternoon is not yet complete on the
    promontory where the victim,
A corporal in the UDR from Lisbellaw, was last seen having
    driven over half
Of Ulster, a legally-held gun was found and the incidence of
    stress came up
On the headland which shadows Larne Harbour and the black
    pitch of warehouses.
There is a melancholy blast of diesel, a puff of smoke which
    might be black or white.
So the harbour slips away to perilous seas as things remain
    unsolved; we listen
To the *ex cathedra* of the fog-horn, and *drink and leave the world
    unseen* −

What's all this to the Belfast business-man who drilled
Thirteen holes in his head with a Black & Decker? It was just
    a normal morning
When they came. The tennis-court shone with dew or frost, a
    little before dawn.
The border, it seemed, was not yet crossed: the Milky Way
    trailed snowy brambles,
The stars clustered thick as blackberries. They opened the door
    into the dark:
The murmurous haunt of flies on summer eves. Empty jam-jars.
Mish-mash. Hotch-potch. And now you rub your eyes and get
    acquainted with the light
A dust of something reminiscent drowses over the garage smell
    of creosote,
The concrete: blue clouds in porcelain, a paint-brush steeped in
    a chipped cup;
Staples hyphenate a wet cardboard box as the upturned can
    of oil still spills
And the unfed cat toys with the yin-yang of a tennis-ball,
    debating whether *yes* is *no*.

50

Serial

As the Guinness-like chiaroscuro of the cat settled into the
   quickthorn hedge
I had a feeling I'd been there before: in a black taxi, for
   example, when this bullet
Drilled an invisible bee-line through the open window and
   knocked a chip
Off the Scotch sandstone façade of the Falls Road Library.
   Everybody ducked
To miss the already-dead split-second; the obvious soldier
   relaxed back into
His Guinness-and-tan uniform, since to hear the shot is to
   know you are alive.

It is this lapse of time which gives the film its serial quality: the
   next
Episode is about the giant statue of the newly-renovated
   Carson, verdigris becoming
Bronze. It is suggested that it might be camouflage – as glossed
   on
In the SF novels of W. D. Flackes, particularly in
   his novel, *The X*
People. And so in the words of another commentator, *the future is
   only today*
Fading into the past – drawing, perhaps, a retrospective dotted
   line on the map

For from here the border makes a peninsula of the South,
   especially in the shallows
Of Lough Erne, where so much land is so much water anyway.
   And, since the Ormsby
Room in Lakeland still remains un-named, they are thinking of
   calling it
Something else: not a name, but the name of a place. Blacklion,
   for instance.

The Blacklion Room has a certain sort of armorial flavour which would suit
The tourist junkets, the loops and spirals of an Irish dancing costume.

Waterfowlers in ulsters, mackintoshes, flak jackets, tank-tops, wade in
Through the rushes and ignore the German fishermen trapped in the caves of Boho.
The water-level is neither here nor there: as they say, *it's making up its mind*
To rain, the grey brainy mass of the clouds becoming cabbages, since a foot patrol
Has just gone over to the other side: you can identify them by the black markings
On their cheeks, the fact that it is winter and the hedges are bare.

These errors of reading are not the only difference between us and them
Though the shibboleths are *lingua franca*, since German became current.
As for Irish, it was too identifiable as foreign: a museum where the stuffed
Wolfhound was just as native as the Shell tiger – I am hunting with a telephoto
Fish-eye, shooting, as they say, some footage. The crackly static
Of the portable still gives some news, though, in between the magazines:

I am hearing a lot, for example, of this campaign to save the English frog.

Refrigerators stocked with spawn are humming quietly in wait;
    the light
Goes off with a click as you shut the door. The freezing dark
    suggests
That they are dying anyway, perplexed by their bi-focal
    vision, as next week,
Or the last week, are the same, and nothing can be justified
As the independent eye of the chameleon sees blue as green.

Asylum

The first indication was this repeated tic, the latch jigging and
  clicking
As he rehearsed the possibility of entering, or opening. Maybe
It was a knock, a question; Uncle John was not all there. Yet he
  had
His father's eyes, his mother's nose; and I myself, according to
  my mother,
Had his mouth. I would imagine speaking for him sometimes.
  He had
A second cousin's hands, or a cousin's twice removed, an
  uncle's way of walking:
In other words, he was himself. So he might walk in this very
  minute, or turn
His back on us to contemplate the yellow brick edgings of the
  bricked-in
Windows of the mill wall opposite. He seemed to see things
  that we didn't
See: cloud-shadow eddying and swirling round a manhole; the
  bits of grit
That glittered at the edges; individual as dirt, the dog-leg walk
  of a dog
As it followed its nose from one side of the street to the other.
  His ears
Might prick to the clatter of an empty tin kicked down an entry,
Diminishing the yelps of children as their skipping rope became
  a blur,
Then slowed and stopped, then whipped back up again, the
  up-hill down-dale
Quickening pulse of a cardiograph. We watched him hover and
  dilate
In the frosted glass. Someone would get up; he would retreat.
  An electric
Yellow bakery van hummed by; he sniffed the air. A car
  backfired.

Like the fast-forward or the rewind button, everything is
   going far too
Fast, though we might know precisely, having heard it all
   before for real,
What is going on, like that climactic moment of a rounded,
   oratorical
Gesture, practised in the mirror till it seemed completely
   unfamiliar:
The hyped-up, ninety-to-the-dozen commentary that
   illustrates, in retrospect,
The split-second when a goal is scored; the laid-back, bit-by-bit
   analysis
As we take in every slowed-down motion of the replay. We are
   looking
For a piece we know is there, amongst the clutter and the glug
   of bottles,
Whispering, the chink of loose change, the unfamiliar voices
   that are us
And cloud our hearing. The repeated melancholic parp of a
   car-horn
Eventually has heralded the moment: now we know what's
   coming next, the voice
Hoarsened by the second-generation tape, the echo of a
   nearly-empty dusty
Concert-hall, illuminated, we imagine, by the voice, one
   shaft of fitful sunlight
That retreated almost instantly to a nimbo-cumulus – gold-
   edged, slate-blue,
Glimmering between its cup and lip – imponderably weighing
   on the skylight.
A yellow bakery van hums by. There is a lull, and then a car
   backfires.

It's getting nearer now, that out-of-focus look he had: a wall-eye

With its yellowed white, the confused rainbow of the iris
    weeping unpredictably.
The tortoise-shell frame had one missing lens. Why they were
    bi-focals
I don't know; he didn't read. Spinning yarns was more his line,
    always something
Off the top of his head. Or he might sing a song: perhaps *I'm
    going down the town*
*And I know who's going with me. I have a wee boy of my own, and his
    name is —*
Here he'd mention my name, which was almost my name; half
    of it, at least,
Was right. All this while he champed, between gulps of tea,
    two thick buttered
Doorsteps of a *Peter Pan* loaf, and cast his eye on the yellowed
    pages
Of an *Old Moore's Almanac* for 1948, the year, in fact, that I was
    born.
Storms this month, I see; hurricanes and thunder . . . the almanac
    was upside down,
But sure enough, just then, above the smoke-stack of the mill
    on up the street,
I caught a dark umbilicus of cloud, a momentary flash. Rain
    pattered on the window.
A yellow bakery van went by; he sniffed the ozone. A car
    backfired.

You can tell that this was all some time ago, although it does
    repeat itself.
On this particular day, my other uncle, Pat, had just come in
    from work.
He plunked two loaves down on the table. A doughy-sour
    inveterate smell

Breathed out from him, and as he lifted off the white cloud of
his cap, it sparked off
The authoritative onset of this other, needle-in-the-haystack
day that I
Began with. That ratchety delay with which the clock is poised,
conjugating
All its tensed-up coils and springs: rain pattered on the
window. An electric
Yellow bakery van whirred off. A car backfired. Someone
seemed to get up very
Slowly. A dog was barking. The car backfired again. Every-
thing was getting faster

And the door bursts open. He is babbling, stammering,
contractions
Getting nearer, nearer, all the blips run into one another till
they are
A wave, a wall: *They said to push, she pushed, they said to shut her
mouth,*
She pushed, they said to keep her head down, and she pushed once more –
The wave has almost broken – *more, they said*: a lock of hair, a
bald patch,
Hair again. Flecks of blood and foam. He cannot get it all out
fast enough.

Afterwards, a lull. He sits up and he takes a cup of tea, a slice of
toast.
He is himself again, though I can see myself in him. *I remember
very well*, he says,
When you were born; oh yes, thunder, hurricanes; and as I see the
bruised
Posthumous violet of his face, I hear him talk about the shape of
this particular

Cloud he saw last week, or this dog he'd noticed last week,
   which he'd imitate,
Panting, slabbering and heaving as it lolled about the margins
   of the new estate –
Nettles, yellow chickweed, piss-the-beds – sniffing, wagging,
   following itself
Back through that remembered day of complex perfume, a trail
   of moments
Dislocated, then located. This dog. That bitch. There is a
   long-forgotten
Whimper, a groan of joy as it discovers home: a creosoted
   hutch, a bowl,
The acrid spoor of something that was human.

Patchwork

It was only just this minute that I noticed the perfectly triangular
Barbed wire rip in the sleeve of my shirt, and wondered where I'd got it.
I'd crossed no fences that I knew about. Then it struck me: an almost identical
Tear in my new white Sunday shirt, when I was six. My mother, after her initial
Nagging, stitched it up. But you can never make a perfect job on tears like that.
Eventually she cut it up for handkerchiefs: six neatly-hemmed squares.
Snags of greyish wool remind me of the mountain that we climbed that day –
Nearly at the summit, we could see the map of Belfast. My father stopped
For a cigarette, and pointed out the landmarks: Gallaher's tobacco factory,
Clonard Monastery, the invisible speck of our house, lost in all the rows
And terraces and furrows, like this one sheep that's strayed into the rags
And bandages that flock the holy well. A little stack of ball-point pens,
Some broken spectacles, a walking-stick, two hearing-aids: prayers
Repeated and repeated until granted.
                             So when I saw, last week, the crucifix
Ear-ring dangling from the right ear of this young Charismatic
Christian fiddle-player, I could not help but think of beads, beads
Told over and over – like my father's rosary of olive stones from

Mount Olive, I think, that he had thumbed and fingered so
    much, the decades
Missed a pip or two. The cross itself was ebony and silver, just
    like
This young girl's, that swung and tinkled like a thurible. She
    was playing
The Teetotaller. Someone had to buy a drink just then, of course:
    a pint of Harp,
Four pints of stout, two Paddy whiskies, and a bottle of
    Lucozade – the baby
Version, not the ones you get in hospital, wrapped in crackling
    see-through
Cellophane. You remember how you held it to the light, and
    light shone through?
The opposite of Polaroids, really, the world filmed in dazzling
    sunshine:
A quite unremarkable day of mist and drizzle. The rainy hush
    of traffic,
Muted car-horns, a dog making a dog-leg walk across a zebra
    crossing . . .
As the lights changed from red to green and back to red again
I fingered the eighteen stitches in the puckered mouth of my
    appendicectomy.

The doctor's waiting room, now that I remember it, had a
    print of *The Angelus*
Above the fireplace; sometimes, waiting for the buzzer, I'd hear
    the Angelus
Itself boom out from St Peter's. With only two or three
    deliberate steps
I could escape into the frame, unnoticed by the peasant and
    his wife. I'd vanish
Into sepia. The last shivering bell would die on the wind.

I was in the surgery. Stainless steel and hypodermics glinted
  on the shelves.
Now I saw my mother: the needle shone between her thumb
  and finger, stitching,
Darning, mending: the woolly callous on a sock, the unravelled
  jumper
That became a scarf. I held my arms at arms' length as she
  wound and wound:
The tick-tack of the knitting needles made a cable-knit pullover.
Come Christmas morning I would wear it, with a new white
  shirt unpinned
From its cardboard stiffener.
                                    I shivered at the touch of cold
  white linen –
A mild shock, as if, when almost sleeping, you'd dreamt you'd
  fallen
Suddenly, and realised now, you were awake: the curtains
  fluttered
In the breeze across the open window, exactly as they had
  before. Everything
Was back to normal. Outside, the noise of children playing: a
  tin can kicked
Across a tarred road, the whip-whop of a skipping-rope,
  singing –
Poor Toby is dead and he lies in his grave, lies in his grave, lies in his
  grave . . .
So, the nicotine-stained bone buttons on my father's melodeon
  clicked
And ticked as he wheezed his way through *Oft in the Stilly Night* –
  or,
For that matter, *Nearer My God to Thee*, which he'd play on
  Sundays, just before
He went to see my granny, after Mass. Sometimes she'd be sick
  – another

Clean shirt'll do me – and we'd climb the narrow stair to where
    she lay, buried
Beneath the patchwork quilt.
                               It took me twenty years to make
    that quilt –
I'm speaking for her, now – and, *your father's stitched into that*
    quilt,
Your uncles and your aunts. She'd take a sip from the baby
    Power's
On the bedside table. *Anything that came to hand, a bit of cotton*
    print,
A poplin tie: I snipped them all up. I could see her working in the
    gloom,
The shadow of the quilt draped round her knees. A needle
    shone between
Her thumb and finger. Minutes, hours of stitches threaded
    patiently; my father
Tugged at her, a stitch went wrong; she started up again. *You*
    drink your tea
Just like your father: two sups and a gulp: and so, I'd see a mirror
    image
Raise the cup and take two sips, and swallow, or place my cup
    exactly on
The brown ring stain on the white damask tablecloth.
                                       Davy's
    gone to England,
Rosie to America; who'll be next, I don't know. Yet they all came
    back.
I'd hardly know them now. The last time I saw them all
    together, was
The funeral. As the rosary was said, I noticed how my father
    handled the invisible
Bead on the last decade: a gesture he'd repeat again at the
    graveside.

A shower of hail: far away, up on the mountain, a cloud of
    sheep had scattered
In the Hatchet Field. *The stitches show in everything I've made,*
    she'd say –
The quilt was meant for someone's wedding, but it never got
    that far.
And some one of us has it now, though who exactly I don't
    know.